Georgia, My State
Biographies

Jackie Robinson

by Doraine Bennett

STATE STANDARDS PUBLISHING LLC

Your State • Your Standards • Your Grade Level

Dear Educators, Librarians and Parents . . .

Thank you for choosing the *"Georgia, My State" Biographies* series! We have designed this series to support the Georgia Department of Education's Georgia Performance Standards for second grade social studies. Each book in the series has been written at appropriate grade level as measured by the ATOS Readability Formula for Books (Accelerated Reader), the Lexile Framework for Reading, and the Fountas & Pinnell Benchmark Assessment System for Guided Reading, and has been evaluated by a reading program consultant to ensure grade-level appropriateness. Photographs and/or illustrations, captions, time line and other design elements have been included to provide supportive visual messaging to enhance text comprehension. Glossary and Word Index sections introduce key new words and help young readers develop skills in locating and combining information. A reproducible Teacher's Guide, available separately, provides opportunities for expanded supervised learning experiences. We wish you all success in using the *"Georgia, My State" Biographies* series to meet your student or child's learning needs. For additional sources of information, see www.georgiaencyclopedia.org.

Jill Ward, President

Publisher
State Standards Publishing, LLC
1788 Quail Hollow
Hamilton, GA 31811
USA
1.866.740.3056
www.statestandardspublishing.com

Library of Congress Cataloging-in-Publication Data
Bennett, Doraine, 1953-
Jackie Robinson / by Doraine Bennett.
p. cm. -- (Georgia, my state biographies)
Includes bibliographical references and index.
ISBN-13: 978-1-935077-04-6 (hardcover)
ISBN-10: 1-935077-04-X (hardcover)
ISBN-13: 978-1-935077-11-4 (pbk.)
ISBN-10: 1-935077-11-2 (pbk.)
1. Robinson, Jackie, 1919-1972--Juvenile literature. 2. Baseball players--United States--Biography--Juvenile literature. 3. African American baseball players--Biography--Juvenile literature. I. Title.
GV865.R6B46 2008
796.357092--dc22
[B] 2008028941

Printed in the United States of America, North Mankato, Minnesota, May 2010, 050710.

2 3 4 5 6 – CG – 14 13 12 11 10

Table of Contents

Jackie Robinson was born in Georgia.

TimeLine

1919
Born

Jackie Robinson

Jackie Robinson was born in Cairo, Georgia in 1919. His father worked on a white farmer's land. He did not have money for his own farm. Jackie's father left when Jackie was one year old. The farmer told Jackie's mother to leave, too.

Jackie and the other boys did harmful things.

TimeLine

1919 Born

1920 Moves to California

Jackie's mother moved her family to California in 1920. African Americans were treated unfairly in California, too. Jackie didn't like being treated unfairly. It made him angry. He joined a **gang**. The boys threw rocks at cars. They painted their names on buildings. This made his mother sad.

Jackie was the first student at UCLA to play four sports in the same year.

TimeLine

1919 Born

1920 Moves to California

1939 Plays sports for UCLA

Good Choices

Jackie loved sports. He decided to join a team instead of the gang. It was a good choice. He went to college at the University of California at Los Angeles (UCLA). He played baseball, football, and basketball. He also ran track.

Jackie served his country in the army.

TimeLine

1919 Born
1920 Moves to California
1939 Plays sports for UCLA
1942 Joins army

Jackie went into the army when he was 23. He became an **officer**. He worked to gain African American soldiers their **rights**. He believed black soldiers should be treated the same as white soldiers.

This is a Negro Leagues baseball team like the one Jackie played on.

TimeLine

1919 Born

1920 Moves to California

1939 Plays sports for UCLA

1942 Joins army

1945 Starts Baseball career

A Baseball Dream

After he left the army, Jackie played baseball in the **Negro Leagues**. His team was the Kansas City Monarchs. But Jackie wanted to play in the **Major Leagues**.

Jackie played for the Brooklyn Dodgers in the Major Leagues.

TimeLine

- 1919 Born
- 1920 Moves to California
- 1939 Plays sports for UCLA
- 1942 Joins army
- 1945 Starts Baseball career

Jackie met Branch Rickey. Mr. Rickey owned the Brooklyn Dodgers. He wanted Jackie to play on his team. No other African American played in the Major Leagues. Mr. Rickey told Jackie that white players and fans would be unkind to him. He asked Jackie not to fight back. Jackie agreed.

1947
Joined the Major Leagues

Jackie's teammates liked having him on the team.

TimeLine

1919	1920	1939	1942	1945
Born	Moves to California	Plays sports for UCLA	Joins army	Starts Baseball career

White fans and players called Jackie names. Some sent him mean letters. Jackie did not fight back. Jackie's teammates liked him. They stood up for him. Jackie was a very good player. He won the **Most Valuable Player** award.

Jackie slides into home plate.

TimeLine

1919 Born

1920 Moves to California

1939 Plays sports for UCLA

1942 Joins army

1945 Starts Baseball career

Jackie came back to Georgia with the Dodgers. They played baseball games in Atlanta and Macon. African Americans from Cairo and other Georgia towns filled the ballparks. They wanted to watch Jackie play ball.

1947
Joins the Major Leagues

1949
Named Most Valuable Player

Jackie was voted into the Baseball Hall of Fame.

TimeLine

1919 Born

1920 Moves to California

1939 Plays sports for UCLA

1942 Joins army

1945 Starts Baseball career

An Important Change

Jackie and baseball helped to change the way the world looked at African American people. Jackie was voted into the **Baseball Hall of Fame** in 1962. He was the first African American to play baseball in the Major Leagues.

1947
Joins the Major Leagues

1949
Named Most Valuable Player

1962
Added to Baseball Hall of Fame

Glossary

Baseball Hall of Fame – a museum that honors great baseball players.

gang – a group of people who join together and do things that are against the law.

Major Leagues – the group of baseball teams that white men played on. Jackie Robinson was the first African American man to play in the Major Leagues.

Most Valuable Player – an award given to the best baseball player on a team or in a league.

Negro Leagues – a group of teams that were made to let African American men play baseball.

officer – a person who leads a group of men and women in the Army.

rights – treating a person in a fair and good way.

Word Index

Image Credits

Cover	Library of Congress, LOOK Magazine Photograph Collection, ppmsc 00047
p. 4	Library of Congress, LOOK Magazine Photograph Collection, ppmsc 00047
p. 6	Copyright © KAR, Fotolia.com
p. 8	© Bettmann/CORBIS
p. 10	© CORBIS
p. 12	© Lucien Aigner/CORBIS
p. 14	© Bettmann/CORBIS
p. 16	© Bettmann/CORBIS
p. 18	© Bettmann/CORBIS
p. 20	© Bettmann/CORBIS

Editorial Credit

Designer: Michael Sellner, Corporate Graphics, North Mankato, Minnesota

About the Author

Doraine Bennett has a degree in professional writing from Columbus State University in Columbus, Georgia and has been writing and teaching writing for over twenty years. She has authored numerous articles in magazines for both children and adults and is the editor of the National Infantry Association's *Infantry Bugler* magazine. Doraine enjoys reading and writing books and articles for children. She lives in Georgia with her husband, Cliff.